My Little Book of
DINOSAURS

by Eileen Daly
illustrated by Rod Ruth

MERRIGOLD PRESS • NEW YORK

Text © 1973 Merrigold Press. Illustrations © 1973 by Rod Ruth.
All rights reserved. Printed in the U.S.A. No part of this book may
be reproduced or copied in any form without written permission
from the publisher. All trademarks are the property of Merrigold
Press, Racine, Wisconsin 53402. ISBN 0-307-17700-9 MCMXCIV

Millions of years ago, Earth was very different from the way it is now. It was warm everywhere. Right where you live, there may have been a jungle or a swamp with a dinosaur in it.

Many dinosaurs laid their eggs in sand. From those eggs came some of the biggest and strangest animals ever to walk the Earth.

Pro-to-CER-a-tops

Di-PLOD-o-cus

There was Diplodocus, the longest land animal that ever lived. It ate several hundred pounds of plants every day to nourish its huge body.

The biggest land animal ever was Brachiosaurus. It was as heavy as a thousand men and looked fearsome—but it wasn't. It had a good way to protect itself, without having to fight.

When an enemy came, Brachiosau-rus could walk into a deep lake, almost to the top of its head, and breathe through nose openings at the very top of its head until the enemy went away.

Brach-i-o-SAU-rus

Brontosaurus was another dinosaur giant. It was peaceable—like Diplodocus and Brachiosaurus—and it liked to stand in the water and eat plants.

Bron-to-SAU-rus

Ty-ran-no-SAU-rus Rex

Some dinosaurs were very fierce. Tyrannosaurus Rex was fiercest of them all. Nothing that lived was safe from it.

Its mammoth head held many sword-like teeth, and it had sharp, strong claws, the only weapons it needed.

TRACH-o-don

Other dinosaurs had strange and unusual heads.

Trachodon had a bill that looked like a duck's, except that it had teeth —about two thousand of them—while a duck has no teeth at all.

Some dinosaurs looked frightful, but they were really harmless.

Stegosaurus grew rows of bony armor along its back—and four bony spikes on its tail—to keep it safe from enemies.

Ste-go-SAU-rus

Sty-ra-co-SAU-rus

Styracosaurus always had to face an enemy, because it grew its armor on its head. It wore a collar of spikes, and a large horn grew on its snout.

Tri-CER-a-tops

Triceratops had three horns like swords, with a great bony shield behind them. Its name means "three horns on the face."

Not all dinosaurs were giants. Compsognathus was only the size of a rooster. It could run very fast on its hind legs to catch its food.

Comp-SOG-na-thus

O-vi-RAPT-or

Oviraptor was small, too. It ate eggs and insects and smaller reptiles. Its name means "egg robber."

There were many kinds of dinosaurs millions of years ago. It is exciting to learn about them now by studying their bones and their eggs—and even the footprints they left!

Can you imagine a footprint that's big enough to play in?